5 Easy Steps To Take Control of Your Money

1 Step at a Time

AF810104

By: Del Shawn R. Hayes

5 Easy Steps to Take Control of Your Money 1 Step at a Time is a guide to personal finance. The material herein is offered for informational purposes solely, and without contract or any type of guaranteed. Readers are encouraged to consult with a financial professional when making any major financial decisions.

Designed by Del Shawn R. Hayes and www.Createspace.com

ISBN-10:0692510451

ISBN-13:978-0692510452

Font: Times new Roman

Photo by: MJ Photography, Covington, KY, 2015

DEDICATION

This book is dedicated to my son Ju Jwan. I thank the Lord for blessing me with a son as awesome as you. You give me the strength and faith to move mountains. I pray that I leave a legacy so you can leave it to your children. May in God's time, you will be all of who He has created you to be. May my love for you out last my life in Jesus Name.

TABLE OF CONTENTS

MY STORY

Philippians 4:12 I know what it is to be in need, and I know what it is to have plenty. I have learned the secret of being content in any and every condition, whether well fed or hungry, whether living in plenty or in want. (NIV)

Can I be transparent today?

At an early age, I figured out how money and working went hand in hand. While other kids were out collecting rocks I was collecting pop bottles to cash in for money. Then it went to collecting aluminum cans. Back then, my mother did not believe in giving us an allowance. She believed there was no sense in paying her children to clean a house they made dirty. (Accept my apology son. Now you know why I never gave you an allowance.)

However, I did teach my son that ***money comes from working.*** There is nothing on this earth that is free. Also, I taught him that nothing is handed to you and no one owes you anything.

Take a moment and write down what you learned from your parents that you took into adulthood concerning money? Good or Bad.

1. ______________________________

2. ______________________________

3. ______________________________

Boy, do I miss my Uncle Jack. He always had me lined up with jobs to do for him. Whether it was washing his dishes, running to the corner store, or cleaning out his car. I can hear him yelling now out of his window, "Shit Hook, Shit Hook, (that was one of his nicknames for me) will you go to the store for me? I'll give you fifty cents." Back then fifty cents was a lot of money to me. Do you know how many pieces of Pal Bubble Gum I could buy? It seemed like Uncle Jack always had money, which meant, I had money too. I never could understand why my siblings didn't take advantage of making money, but I wasn't' mad at them at all. That meant more money for me, Shit Hook.

Growing up, Mom, Dad, my sister, and two brothers lived with my grandparents and we lived on a fixed income. We went to the grocery store once a month. Grandma ran a tab at the local neighborhood store for items we would run out of during the month. You can say this was my first experience with a line of credit. Each month she would pay the balance in full and start back over for the following month.

By the time I reached my teenage years, both my grandparents had passed away. Although my mother had a college degree, she was a stay at home wife. As time went on, Mom and Dad separated and we begin to hit rock bottom. The little assistance we did receive did not cover all the bills. I couldn't understand back then why Mom did not go out and get a job. Our gas and electric was shut off and next was the water. I loved my mother but I couldn't understand as a child, why we had to live like that. I can remember we collected roofing shingles and burned them in the fireplace to keep us warm. At night, we carried buckets of water from the neighbor's just to wash up and flush the toilet. I don't know how many bologna sandwiches we had for dinner. We lived like that until my mother ran into her best friend one day and moved us into her two-bedroom apartment. There were eight people in one apartment. A two month stay resulted in a two year stay. It reminded me of the television show Gilligan's Island with their three hour tour ended in being shipwrecked. That's how I felt, Shit Hook was shipwrecked.

The most exciting day was when I turned sixteen. Now I was able to work and make my own money. I could purchase what I needed and when I needed it. I was screaming in the inside, "Shit Hook is back in business!"

My first job was at Burger King. I remember my grandmother saying, "Save for a raining day." That's when I opened my first bank account. Twenty plus years later, I'm still a customer of that same bank.

By my senior year, we moved into our own apartment and things started looking up. My mother had full-time employment. I was so happy. No longer did she have to rely on fake promises from boyfriends or her children's fathers. Although my mother was now working, we had our responsibility in the household. I had the responsibility of paying the phone bill. So you know I wasn't going for the long distance phone calls from anyone expect my mother.

The following year after graduation, I had my handsome son. I was a single parent with one income trying to make ends meet. This wasn't how I plan my life to be. But I was determined, that no matter what, my child would always have shelter, food, electricity, and water. Although I received child support I never relied on it. I never forgot where I came from and I did not want to go back or let my child experience what I went through.

Each month as I saw my grandmother do, I would get my pencil and paper and sit at the kitchen table adding up all my bills to pay and their due dates. I figured how much money I needed to bring home every two weeks to see if I had to work overtime or not. I lived in public housing so I didn't have to pay for gas and electric or water. Hallelujah!

As time went on, it got extremely hard catching a bus with a baby and a big diaper bag. When tax season came around, I took all of my tax refund and applied it to a down payment on a car. I bought a light blue 1980 Ford Mustang from a Pay Here Buy Here lot. Every two weeks I paid $75.00 until it was paid in full. I was so proud. I was driving a car that belonged to me and I owed no one.

Meanwhile, I continued at Burger King working my way up to becoming an Assistance Manager. As the years went on I begin to establish credit and that meant credit cards. I had them all! Remember Fingerhut? I had every department store credit card you could think of.

Newsflash! Just because your income increases doesn't mean you can run out and increase your debt. Sitting at the kitchen table with my pencil and paper was no longer my monthly routine. I was too busy shopping, living the life and not planning for my future or my son as a matter of fact. I was reckless with credit. I was living like the Joneses and my last name was Hayes. I would ignore creditor's calls. When I did answer, I would lie and say, "Mr. Del isn't here." As long as I had a roof over my head, food, and transportation, I was okay. But in reality I was not. I was a runner!

In addition to debt, I soon jumped back into dating. Hello! Debt and dating don't mix. I met a man I fell madly in love with and we moved in together. A lesson learned - love does not pay the bills. You're talking about someone in love with a man that didn't bring anything to the table but a fork and knife. Already in debt, I was digging myself deeper and deeper. I would pay for everything. If he needed a t-shirt without asking me, I would go out and buy it. When we would go out to eat, I paid. We'd go out of town, I paid. The light bulb still did not come on. I continued to stay in that unhealthy debt digger relationship. I would borrow money from check cashing places to help pay his bills. When I suggested we talk about saving and budgeting, he would brush it off and say, "You only live once and you can't take it with you when you're dead." Each time we would argue about money, to heal the pain I would go shopping. Remember I'm getting deeper and deeper in debt.

Finally one day after work, I came home and my son was doing his normal routine of laying on the floor doing his homework. This time though, the television was not blasting. I questioned him why the television was off. He said, "They cut the lights off." Standing in the living room at that moment took me back to my youth living under a roof with no lights. I was so furious and disappointed in myself for trusting someone other than myself with the responsibility of paying a bill. That living arrangement last three months when I realized I was buying his love. The very next day I made some phone calls and within a month I was back to living single with my son.

In 2002, I begin to prepare to purchase my first home and at this time my credit score was in the four hundreds which meant I owed everyone. I told myself in one year I would buy a house. I went to a home ownership workshop where I learned how to run and understand my credit report, negotiate my debt, budgeting, and savings. It was a long hard process but I had to ***make a move and make it count***. I had to make many sacrifices within that year including, no more eating out, shopping, vacationing and no more cell phone. On August 15, 2003 I moved into my house with this scripture: "Unless the Lord builds a house you labor in vain."

Psalms 127:1 (NIV)

Twelve years later I'm still standing on this scripture.

After all that hard work, my behavior and relationship with money did not change permanently. Although I held degrees in Accounting and understood how money works, I still had some bad spending habits. I still wanted to be there for everyone even when it meant that I did without. All I did was change my behavior temporarily to obtain that specific goal. I began to open up credit card accounts to take vacations and shopping. I was headed back to my old ways although I knew better.

List some of your financial goals. However, your goals are to be specific. For example, I want to save $10,000.00 to purchase my first car or I want to pay off $800.00 in credit card debt.

1. ______________________________

2. ______________________________

3. ______________________________

4. ______________________________________

5. ______________________________________

List some sacrifices you think you will have to make. For example, I will give myself a pedicure at home instead of going to the nail salon every two weeks.

1. ______________________________________

2. ______________________________________

3. ______________________________________

4. ______________________________________

5. ______________________________________

Fast forward 5 years. I had opened my Beauty and Supply store, and then my mother's illness turned for the worst. My relationship was over. My son was heading to college. I felt so lonely and depressed. To think people really thought I had everything together but in reality everything was falling apart. It seems like the nursing home was my second home. I was there more than at work or running my business. While at work, I was barely reaching forty hours each week. I didn't have enough money to cover household or business expenses. I was behind on all bills, even the necessities. I was beginning to receive embarrassing phone calls from creditors at my place of employment. All my walls begin tumbling down. I had to close my business. My 2009 Ford Explorer was repossessed. I was losing weight due to stress. I thought about suicide and all the while I still kept smiling and playing the part that everything was alright. I couldn't let anyone see me not at my "A" game. My pride wouldn't let me tell anyone and if I did tell, who could help me out?

Finally in 2012, I was asked this question, "If I wanted to bless you right now, could you tell me how much debt you owe? When I added up all my debt, I just begin to cry. Next, I begin to go into the "woe is me" mode asking and screaming at God, “Why is this happening to me?” You know the speech we give God. I’m a good person, I pay my tithes, I serve in ministry, I have degrees in accounting, and the list went on. When I stopped having my kiddy fit and wiped my eyes, I heard God say, *“Owe nothing to anyone--except for your obligation to love one another.”* (Roman 13:8 NIV) When I got real with myself about my finances, God began to work on some changes within me. I made a list of all the reasons why I couldn’t save and why I spent money so easy that I did not have. It was hard to do but I did it with tears running down my face. I had to ***make a move and make it count.***

Looking over my list, I knew my mindset about money had to change. My behavior about money had to change. My level of giving of money had to change. My speech about money had to change. I had to do something different so I had to ***Move Something.***

I would not be on my assignment that God has given to me, if I had not taken the time and shared what changed my life and hopes in helping others to change theirs. This book is written based on being God lead, my personal life experiences, and professional experiences. Now, let's begin our road to financial freedom.

Make a list of reasons why you cannot save money.

1. ____

2. ____

3. ____

4. ____

5. ____

Make a list of reasons why you spend money.

1. ____

2. ____

3. ______________________________

4. ______________________________

5. ______________________________

What are your thoughts about money?

1. ______________________________

2. ______________________________

3. ______________________________

4. ______________________________

5. ______________________________

What behaviors do you have towards money that needs to change?

1. ______________________________

2. ______________________________

3. ______________________________

4. ______________________________

5. ______________________________

What are you speaking into the atmosphere concerning money? Are you constantly speaking: "You will always be broke", "You never have any money", and "All you do is pay bills"?

1. ______________________________

2. ______________________________

3. ______________________________

4. ______________________________

5. ______________________________

You have read my story of financial struggles and how I become so passionate about becoming debt free. But before you go any farther, I want you to stop and pat yourself on the back. You have decided to "*make a move and make it count"* when you picked up this book. Its evidence you've already invested in your financial well-being. Inside, you will learn information that will have you moving in the direction of taking control of your money.

Repeat after me!

1. I can be debt free. I will be debt free.
2. I can have a savings. I will have a savings.
3. I can have a marriage with no financial burden. I will have a marriage with no financial burden.
4. I can be a lender and not a borrower. I will be a lender and not a borrower.
5. I can owe no one but love. I will owe no one but love.

Go ahead and write down your personal daily affirmations.

1. ____
   ____
   ____

2. ____

____

____

3. ____

____

____

4. ____

____

____

5. ____

____

____

Repeat your daily affirmations and speak them into existence. I have enough faith in you that you can and will succeed on your debt free financial movement. All you have to do is ***move something.***

CHAPTER 1

BASIC BUDGETING

A Budget! No Way! I know the frustration when you're already struggling to make ends meet, despite working extra-long hours. For every time I throw my hands up in the air trying to budget and failed, I would be rich and debt free. It was hard to stick to $50 on entertainment for the entire month and I wasn't a happy camper staying home on the weekend when the money ran out in week one.

I had to change my thinking and so do you. Don't get in the habit of thinking by having a budget puts life and living on pause. In fact, it does the opposite having a budget helps live a life on your terms. Budgeting can be fun with the right mindset. With a budget, you can play the game of assigning your money where you want it to go; no longer will your money tell you where it goes. But just like anything, in order to know where you are heading you will need a plan, and that means you will need a budget. When you establish a plan make sure it's a plan that's *realistic*. It makes no sense to start a budget without having a goal and plan in mind.

Write 5 goals as to why you need a budget. Be specific.

1.____

2.____

3.____

4.____

5.____

Newsflash! Don't think that a budget is here today and gone tomorrow. A budget is a tool that will help you with your future. It's all about planning. Even those of you with no income at the present time, you will need a budget once the income begins to roll in and I want you to be ready.

Here's a list of reasons why a budget is necessary and helpful.

- Helps you determine whether you can dine out or eat at home.
- Helps you determine whether you can purchase a new pair of shoes or polish up the ones you have.
- Helps you determine whether you can take a trip or stay home.
- Helps you set a target date for your financial goals.
- Helps you not to feel guilty if someone asks you to borrow money and your response is no.
- Helps you become disciplined in your spending.
- Helps you from playing the guessing game on who gets paid next.

Don't get overwhelmed with fancy budget sheets that you see. A basic budget can be created using an excel spreadsheet. If you're old school like me, a pen, paper, and a calculator will work just the same. Trust me, implementing a budget into your household will eliminate unspoken expenses and prevent financial worries.

Sample Budget Sheet

Monthly Gross income $________________

	Budget	Actual	Due Date
Tithes	$______	$______	_______
Rent/Mortgage	$______	$______	_______
Gas/Electric	$______	$______	_______
Water	$______	$______	_______
Sanitation	$______	$______	_______
Phone/Cell Phone	$______	$______	_______
Internet	$______	$______	_______
Cable	$______	$______	_______
Groceries	$______	$______	_______
Car Payment	$______	$______	_______
Gasoline	$______	$______	_______
Car Insurance	$______	$______	_______
Car Maintenance	$______	$______	_______
Student Loans	$______	$______	_______
Credit Card	$______	$______	_______

Day Care	$_____	$_____	______
Life Insurance	$_____	$_____	______
Gym Membership	$_____	$_____	______
House Supplies	$_____	$_____	______
Clothes	$_____	$_____	______
Salon	$_____	$_____	______
Barber	$_____	$_____	______
Savings	$_____	$_____	______
Total Expense:	$_____	$_____	______

Income – Expenses = $_______________

A regular budget should be zero based. Every cent should be assignment. Don't be afraid to tell your money where to go.

Budget Percent Guidelines

Charitable Gifts 10-15%

Savings 5-10%

Housing 25-35%

Utilities 5-10%

Food 5-15%

Transportation 10-15%

Clothing 2-7%

Medical/Health 5-10%

Personal 5-10%

Entertainment 5-10%

Debts 5-10%

Remember you can update your budget anytime.

5 Easy Budget Rules

Rule 1: Add up all of your income

All income includes your net income (take home pay), child support, alimony, any and all monies coming into the household. This number you will use when creating your budget. If all your income adds up to $500 that's the money number to cover all expenses.

Rule: 2: List all your expenses

There are two types of expenses: fixed and variable. Fixed expenses are expenses that do not change over time periods, in other words, it does not fluctuate. Such expenses are your mortgage, car payment or student loans. Variable expense is the opposite. The cost is determined by the usage, rate, and time period. A few examples are gas and electric, water bill, gas for your car and yes, even lunch.

Prioritize your necessary basics expenses first. I like to refer to them as "Paul's kids". Why? People will rob Peter to pay Paul. These necessities are food, housing, transportation, and utilities. Often times we are forced to compromise on the basics. Make sure you list every expense even the $5 you pay little Timmy down the street to cut your grass. Don't forget your seasonal expenses: tanning services, summer clothing, vacation, summer programs, or water park passes. Remember, a budget is personal. When you write everything on paper, this will give you a clear understanding how money is going out the door and where it is going.

Rule 3: Know your due dates

The most important and valuable dates you need to know are the dates you get paid. The second is to know the due dates of your bills. This will keep you from paying late fees that can and will affect your credit report in the future. Return back to Rule 2 when you list all your expenses, make sure you write down the due dates of each one. There is no worse feeling then coming home after a hard day's work and there is no electricity because you were a day late on a payment.

Rule 4: Let technology work for you

There are many available tools that can keep you motivated in budgeting. Most cell phones have apps that will remind you when the bills are due. You can set up automatic withdrawal. Go online and monitor your account regularly.

Here are 5 Money Management Apps

WWW.MINT.COM

WWW.DAILYCOST.COM

WWW.LEARNVEST.COM

WWW.GOODBUDGET.COM

WWW.EVERYDOLLAR.COM

Rule 5: Work the Plan

You may be thinking it is easier said than done. Well, I'm here to tell you if you get sidetrack get **S.O.U. P**. (start over until perfected). Will it be easy? To be honest there will be times you may feel like you're on a roller coaster. Will it get easier? Absolutely!

Again work the plan. You may not be able to control the fixed expenses but you have complete control over the variable. So, if you budget $100 for groceries then don't leave the house without a grocery list and coupons. If you still don't trust yourself take an accountability partner. The word "No" will seem harsh when you want to purchase a want but it will be worth it in the end.

Coupons are Cash

This segment is not about teaching you how to coupon but how it can impact your family budget and increase savings. The most important thing I can't stress more is buy what you need. Let me repeat it again, buy what you need. Having 52 bottles of detergent in your stock pile but no meat in the freezer is not sensible. Sales come along all the time, so again buy what you need. I once heard couponing is evil. But who doesn't like a discount? Who doesn't like free stuff? My philosophy is "if it's free it's for me, if I have to pay it will stay".

Here are some reasons why people use coupons:

- Tight grocery budget.
- Saving money to pay on other debt.
- Donations to a nonprofit organization.
- Help a child away in college.
- Help elderly parents and family members.

Rules for Couponing

1. Always purchase a Sunday paper.
2. Never leave the house without your coupons.
3. Know each store policy.
4. Know the coupon language/code.

5. Never use coupons on full price items.

6. Get a rain check on items that are out of stock.

Couponing isn't as easy as you think and isn't for everybody. It takes time, sacrifice, organization, supplies, and commitment. There were times I spent most of the day clipping coupons and thumbing through newspaper ads to prepare for new sales but all I wanted to do is relax. What kept me motivated was coupons are cash. Coupons are cash! There also were times when I was frustrated when I've arrived at the store and my items were out of stock. Yes, I said my items like I was the only one hipped to couponing. So I would jump back in the car to go to the next store just to burn more gas. But I kept thinking coupons are cash. There are all kinds of ends and outs of couponing but the most important is learning the language code. If you want to learn more about couponing here are some websites to help you along the way.

www.bargaincouponclippers.com

www.couponing101.com

www.krazykouponlady.com

www.moneysavingmom.com

www.weusecoupons.com

What I want for you is to develop a mindset those coupons are cash. Let's take this survey to see how you think about coupons.

1. How often do you use coupons?

A. Weekly.

B. Monthly.

C. Too much hassle.

D. I have money I don't need to use coupons.

2. How many times per month do you go shopping?

A. Once a week.

B. Bi-Weekly.

C. 3-4 times a week.

D. Once a month.

3. What if I told you that couponing can save you an average of $150 a month on your grocery bill, will you begin?

A. I don't know.

B. I don't have the time.

C. It's too much work.

D. Yes.

4. After taking this survey if you're not couponing how soon will you begin?

A. Right away.

B. Next month.

C. 3-6 month.

D. 6-9 month.

Not only coupons are great but don't forget about store rebates, discounts, membership discounts, cash back, awards bucks, and online shopping to name a few. They all play an important part of your savings plan and keep you within your budget.

Remember a budget is not written in solid stone. It will change as your life changes and as debt is decreasing. It will also change as the season changes. During the winter months my gas and electric bill may run $300.00 or higher. Then when summer comes, it drops down to $150.00. A budget is personal. I encourage you to review your budget weekly, monthly or quarterly. This will give you a definite understanding of your financial state.

If you have completed your budget you should have found areas where you needed to cut back in order to free up money. Hello, do you really need that large cable package?

Write them down.

1. ______________________________

2. ____________________

3. ____________________

4. ____________________

5. ____________________

If you tried budgeting before and wasn't successful, I want you to know nothing beats a failure but a try. So, keep trying, but let's be honest, does any of the following statements down below apply to you? If so, place a check mark beside the ones that does.

1. You weren't completely honest and left some things out of your budget. If you leave it out of your budget then this expense will creep up on you.

2. You just don't do the work. Commit to a specific day and time before the month is over to do the work.

3. Your faith begins to weaken. You have to believe that you can. I know you can but you have to believe it for yourself.

4. You went in this thing alone without having an accountability partner.

5. You haven't established the difference from a need and a want.

6. You are living above your means. I'm sorry you may have to downsize to rise up again.

7. You think a budget is a waste of time when the month last longer than your money does.

8. You did not log your spending.

9. Lastly, you did not have this book.

Keep going and remember the reason why you purchased this book so you can live the life you dreamed of.

Daily Spending Log

DATE	Item	Cash or Credit Card	Amount

Daily Spending Log

DATE	Item	Cash or Credit Card	Amount

Chapter 2

Safe Savings

Now that you understand your budget, it's time to implement your savings. In the last chapter I asked you to review your budget to find areas to cut back and free up money. It's time to pay yourself so, get your budget back out and add your name. Don't forget to enter your due date. Ask yourself, do I want to get paid weekly, bi-weekly or monthly. It's time to implement $1,000.00 for your emergency fund. My favorite saying is ***"move something"*** into your savings. I don't care what the dollar amount is as long as you move something into your savings account. If you don't stop, you will get there. I promise you.

For those of you that are frustrated and pulling your hair out this is for you. For years I tried to save money and it seemed impossible. When things went wrong I hit up check cashing establishments to cover unexpected expenses. Even when I scaled my budget as much as I could, I was still unable to save. When I took a close look at my spending journal I saw that I never turned down an opportunity to meet up with friends for dinner and I always gave when I didn't have it. Believe me, you will find a hole in your pocket where your money is going. Pray, look, pray, and look.

Here are some quick tips to help jump start your savings.

1. Set up direct deposit for each pay period and have a certain amount automatically deposited into a savings account that you do not have immediate access to.
2. Deposit your tax refund to your savings.
3. Don't be afraid to use your coins. Go ahead and deposit your coins into your savings. Pennies do add up to dollars.

4. Eat your groceries. The money you normally spend eating out for lunch, deposit that into your savings.
5. Limit your use of your debit or credit card. Don't get in the habit of swiping without balancing your account.
6. Convert to the cash envelope method. Put a set amount in an envelope and once it's gone no more spending. Hello! It doesn't work if you forget to stop by the bank before leaving the house.
7. Stop trying to live like the Joneses. Stop trying to live above your means. Just because you can buy it doesn't' mean you can afford it.
8. Emotional shopping can lead you into debt. So before you go on a shopping spree- PRAY. Shopping gives us the illusion it makes you feel better but it's just a temporary fix.

9. Tell yourself "No." You don't deserve something you can't afford. It will be the hardest thing you can do but remember you have a goal to reach so that means sacrificing a want.
10. Look around the house if you don't need or use something then sell it.
11. Call your creditors to see if you can get a discount if you have been a loyal customer.
12. Never spend your money before you earn it.
13. If you're going to spend, keep your budget and savings journal handy.
14. Get an accountability partner to keep you focused.
15. Stop lending money that you need to build your savings.
16. If you don't need it get rid of it. Yes, I'm talking about cable, internet or that gym membership.
17. Switch to e-bills. Some companies charge a fee to have paper bills mailed to you.

18. Wash your clothes with cold water and when it's a full load of clothes.
19. Drink tap water or invest in a filtration system.
20. Track your spending. The biggest lie you will tell yourself is that you will remember at the end of the month. So, write down your spending daily.

My all-time favorite is the 52 week savings plan. I implemented this in my budget for the last three years. I tell you it works. How it works: You save something each week starting the 1st week of the year. You save $1 the 1st week and increase it by a dollar each week for 52 weeks. Your savings should be$1,378.00 at end of the year.

Week	Deposit Amt.	ACCT BAL
1	$ 1.00	$ 1.00
2	$ 2.00	$ 3.00
3	$ 3.00	$ 6.00
4	$ 4.00	$ 10.00
5	$ 5.00	$ 15.00
6	$ 6.00	$ 21.00
7	$ 7.00	$ 28.00

8	$	8.00	$	36.00
9	$	9.00	$	45.00
10	$	10.00	$	55.00
11	$	11.00	$	66.00
12	$	12.00	$	78.00
13	$	13.00	$	91.00
14	$	14.00	$	105.00
15	$	15.00	$	120.00
16	$	16.00	$	136.00
17	$	17.00	$	153.00
18	$	18.00	$	171.00
19	$	19.00	$	190.00
20	$	20.00	$	210.00
21	$	21.00	$	231.00
22	$	22.00	$	253.00
23	$	23.00	$	276.00
24	$	24.00	$	300.00
25	$	25.00	$	325.00
26	$	26.00	$	351.00
27	$	27.00	$	378.00
28	$	28.00	$	406.00
29	$	29.00	$	435.00
30	$	30.00	$	465.00
31	$	31.00	$	496.00
32	$	32.00	$	528.00
33	$	33.00	$	561.00
34	$	34.00	$	595.00
35	$	35.00	$	630.00
36	$	36.00	$	666.00
37	$	37.00	$	703.00
38	$	38.00	$	741.00
39	$	39.00	$	780.00
40	$	40.00	$	820.00
41	$	41.00	$	861.00
42	$	42.00	$	903.00
43	$	43.00	$	946.00
44	$	44.00	$	990.00
45	$	45.00	$	1,035.00
46	$	46.00	$	1,081.00
47	$	47.00	$	1,128.00

48	$	48.00	$	1,176.00
49	$	49.00	$	1,225.00
50	$	50.00	$	1,275.00
51	$	51.00	$	1,326.00
52	$	52.00	$	1,378.00

Write Down 20 Ways You Can Jump Start Your Savings.

1. ____

2. ____

3. ____

4. ____

5. ____

6. ____

7. ____

8. ____

9. ____

10. ____

11. ____

12. ____

13. ____

14. ____

15. ____

16. ____

17. ____

18. ____

19. ____

20. ____

Saving money is the number one key to building wealth and becoming a debt free consumer. Once you begin saving, make sure you place your savings into an account you do not have immediate access to. This will prevent you from dipping in your savings. Also have two separate accounts one for bills and other for savings.

Chapter 3

Cash after College

Congratulations. You have accomplished a milestone. No more classes and no more exams. What a relief I'm sure. But don't get too comfortable, there is still work to be done. Did you know six months after graduating repayment on student loans begins? Yikes! Don't get overwhelmed, it may take time but you can do it.

Here are some quick tips to help you jump start to begin a savings for repayment.

- Ask for monetary gifts for graduating. You can use this money towards your first payment.
- Move in with your parents until you have a job that will cover your student loans.
- Sell your stuff.

- Turn your passion into extra income. If you're good at drawing then sell your artwork.

When I graduated with my Bachelor's degree I had over $48,000.00 of student loan debt. I remember crying at the kitchen table. By now you can see a pattern that everything is done at my kitchen table. Not only did I have my current household expenses, now I accrued an additional $400 to my budget without an increase in pay. I had to pull back out my budget and see what areas to cut costs. I trimmed down as much as I could.

One of my biggest mistakes that I regret was not taking advantage of the college tuition reimbursement my employer offered and I wouldn't have been an extra $12k in debt. The way my mind was thinking, if I commit to this agreement and decided to leave the company after graduation, before the given time period, I would have to repay the company back the money. You can see my thinking was way off. It would have made sense to stay another two years and walk away not owing anyone any money at all. The sad part is I'm still at the same company three years later. Don't make the same mistake as I did.

Next, my only solution was to begin working a second job. I went from working forty hours to eighty hours a week to cover expenses. Is this the way for everyone? Absolutely not! But you have to ask yourself how bad you want to get out of debt.

When I started paying on my student loans all I heard from friends was put your loans in deferment or forbearance. Sounds great, but they fail to realize that my student loans continue to collect interest even in forbearance. When you hear this, remember that you are taking a step towards controlling your money. One of my friends said, "As long as I can keep my loans in deferment, I will and I'm not thinking about paying them back." This is not the way to go. I encourage you to own up to your debt, and then pay it off so you can live the life you want.

So, if you don't have a budget the time is now to create one and refer back to Chapter 2. Remember to make an effective and realistic plan; you will need to know the following so I suggest that you revisit the exit counseling on www.studentloans.gov if you received federal loans. This will help you answer some of the questions listed below.

1. Do you know how much you owe in student loans?

____

2. Do you know the type of loans you have? Subsidized vs. Unsubsidized.

____

3. Do you know if your interest is fixed?

____

4. Do you qualify for an income-based repayment plan?

____

No more student loans will free you up to having a life on your terms. So the faster you pay off your student loans the less interest you have to pay.

Here are some ways to pay off your student loans faster.

1. If you can pay your student loans bi-weekly do so. This way you are paying less interest because there is less time payments for interest to accrue.

2. Throw all of your extra money into your student loan. That bonus and especially your tax return. Look at it as if it was money you didn't have. The quicker you pay off your loans the quicker you can enjoy your bonuses and tax returns in the future.

3. If you have extra money put it towards the loan with the highest interest rate.

4. Consolidate your loans only if your new interest rate is lower than your original. Remember the more you consolidate the longer it is to pay down your loan. So refer to steps 1 & 2.

5. Get a part-time job. All the checks from your part time job will go directly to pay off your student loans.

6. Sign Up for Direct Debt. It's an automated payment service that if you qualify for a 0.25% interest rate reduction.

7. Check on loan forgiveness programs or careers that will pay for your student loans.

8. See if your employer will reimburse your education so that you can pay off student loans.

Remember student loans are real debts.

Here are some consequences for non-payment.

- Your wages will be garnished
- Your tax refunds can be taken.
- Affects your credit.
- You'll lose social security benefits.

List some ways to pay off your student loans.

1. ______________________________________

____

____

2. ______________________________________

____

____

3.

4.

5.

6.

7.

Chapter 4

Decreasing Debt

Say this three times and each time I want you to get louder than before, "It's not how much I earn but what I keep that will help pay down my debt".

The reason why I had you to do that exercise is to let you know unless you take control of your spending and maintain your budget, no matter how much money you make it will not help you get out of debt. I remembered working two full time jobs and still was in debt just spending and not sticking to my plan.

I don't want you to become the hamster on a wheel just going in circles paying off the balances of your credit cards just to max them out again. Stop picking up the same debt. Just because a store has a sale doesn't mean you need to go shopping.

Paying off debt not only gives you financial freedom, it has also promoted behavior and a mindset change. You will be amazed on how your behavior changes once you start paying down debt. I can remember walking around grumpy and moody knowing I had all this debt on my back. Instead of looking up, my head was always down. When the Pastor talked about money and tithes I would grumble under my breath. As time went on, one debt was paid in full then my smile and the pep in my steps started coming back. After that I knew, I could live the life I always wanted.

Are you ready to ***make your move and make it count?*** It's time to tackle debt head on.

List reasons why you are in debt and be honest.

1.____

2.____

3.____

4.____

5.____

6.____

7.____

8. _______________________________________

9. _______________________________________

10.______________________________________

Newsflash! ***You can't attack debt you don't know you have.*** It's time to run that credit report! Here are two companies that will give you access to a free credit report.

www.freeannualreport.com

www.creditkarma.com

Once you have your credit report review it with a fine tooth comb. Every detail on your credit report is vital. Make sure everything that is on your credit report is accurate and it belongs to you. People are known to have information on their credit report that was not their debt. I advise everyone to run a credit report twice a year. I wouldn't want anything inaccurate on your credit report that prevents you from purchasing a home or getting that dream job. I mentioned a job because more and more employers are running credit reports on potential candidates for employment.

Always contact each creditor by mail requesting a verification letter that you owe the debt before contacting via telephone. This way you can have the debt in front of you. Once you receive proof of the debt, pull out your budget and savings journal. Then figure how much money you can afford to fit into your budget. Remember as you're paying down debt, don't stop saving. Paying down debt and savings should be simultaneously. If an emergency occurs without having a savings either you go back to swiping your credit card or borrowing additional money to cover the emergency cost.

Now when it's time to make those calls do not begin negotiating. Most creditors want some form of payment. Call them and be honest and explain that you would like to resolve the issue but your financial condition is limited. Most if not all will offer you discounts, settlements, or a payment plan to resolve it. I can't stress this enough, *never* commit to a payment that you cannot afford. If you can only afford to pay $50 monthly, let them know up front. When you do come to an agreement, get it in writing and never give them access to your bank account.

Many experts advise people to pay down the highest interest rate or highest balance first and work your way down. That is wonderful, but if you're like me, I love instant gratification. What I've found to keep me motivated to pay off debt consistently is to pay the lowest balance first. It was easier for me to knock out that $200 Macy's credit card than that $2,000.00 Sam's card. Do you see where I'm heading? I saw the results faster that kept my momentum going. It worked for me and I know it will work for you. Don't get overwhelmed, frustrated, or discouraged. **Getting out of debt is a process**.

However, one of the most important keys is to surround yourself with those on the same mission as you. Facebook has a support group that will help encourage you when you can't see the light at the end of the tunnel. Just reading other's posts will give you the drive to continue when you feel like giving up.

Make a list of all your debt and balances from smallest to largest.

Creditor Name	Balance
1.______________	$______________
2.______________	$______________
3.______________	$______________
4.______________	$______________

5.________________ $_______________

6.________________ $_______________

7. _______________ $_______________

8.________________ $_______________

9.________________ $_______________

10.______________ $_______________

Once I paid off one debt I begin the snowball method. What's the snowball method? It's when you are paying on one or more debts at the same time. When one of the debts is paid off, you will take that money and tackle the other.

Here's your opportunity to try snowballing. Take the four lowest debts and pay the minimum on each. Once one is paid off you use that amount to pay off the other.

Debt	Amount	Min. Payment
________	________	____________
________	________	____________
________	________	____________
________	________	____________

Which plan is right for you? It's the same as a budget when it comes to paying down debt. It's personal. Just remember that your debt did not occur overnight and it will go away in time if you commit to your plan and making every move count.

As you continue the process of becoming debt free and build wealth this will also prepare you to teach your children on the importance of their relationship with money. Then your children will teach their children. You will leave a legacy of financial wellness.

Here are things to consider for your children.

- If you want to send your children to college begin to save now so your children will not be bombarded with student loan debt. When you don't plan you are setting your children up. College is expensive, so create a college fund. Research the 529 College savings plan.

- Learn to tell your children "No". They cannot always have everything they want in the store.

- Every dollar they get for birthday is not to be spent. Teach them how to save.

- Money comes from working. Teaching them that money doesn't come from mommy and daddy but by working.

- Don't get in the habit of teaching them that they need the latest and greatest technology.

Chapter 5

Marriage & Money

You've gone from being single with no accountability on the way you spent your money to having a partner to hold you accountable. This can be frustrating. For some of us, this is a dramatic mind and behavior change. Your money is no longer your money. His money is not your money. Her money is not your money. However, all money is both of your money.

Here's a reality check, your spouse is not your financial plan. Hopefully by the time you said, "I do" that during your engagement stage you and your spouse went over each other's financials. If not, the time is now to lay it all on the kitchen table.

Having a financial conversation should have taken place doing courtship and definitely doing the engagement. It can be uncomfortable for both parties. What seems important to you may not seem like it's important to him or her. When I asked questions I received attitude with the answers. I learned that my ex-fiancés mindset wasn't on the road to becoming debt free. When I asked to see a credit report it was always a reason why it wasn't brought to the table. I soon realized that shame was a part of the debt. Some of the reasons of being in debt were due to poor spending habits, poor budgeting, and not enough income coming in. When communicating with one another, present a sensitive, understanding, and encouraging attitude to ensure that the two of you will be on the same page.

Keep in mind that marriage is a partnership. So, be honest upfront. This will avoid the money fights in the marriage if you know what each other's debt carried into the marriage. Share with each other so you both can make a plan in becoming debt free. The right hand should always know what the left hand is doing. Your wedding vows were for richer and poorer. But, who really married to live poorer?

Answer the following questions to see if you're on the same money steps to success:

1. **Should each spouse have separate or joint savings or checking account?**

    A. Yes.

    B. No.

    C. Don't Know.

    D. I love you, but I have trust issues with my money.

2. **Who will do the budgeting for the household?**

    A. Wife.

    B. Husband.

    C. Don't Know.

    D. What's the point in a budget we know who we owe?

3. **Should all the bills be divided equally if one spouse's income is higher than the other?**

   A. Yes, the spouse with the higher income pays all bills.

   B. No, each bill will be divided straight down the middle.

   C. Don't know.

   D. One spouse for the major household expenses and other pays for minor expenses.

4. **Should all major purchases be discussed with each spouse prior to buying?**

   A. No, it's my money.

   B. Yes, we are a team.

   C. We will sit down and discuss.

D. Don't know.

5. **How often will you meet to go over the budget and balancing the checkbook?**

   A. Once a week.

   B. Monthly.

   C. Quarterly.

   D. Yearly.

6. **How would you treat additional income, such as yearly bonus checks or tax returns?**

   A. Go Shopping.

   B. Pay Down Debt.

   C. Move to Savings.

   D. Vacation.

7. How much money each pay period will go into a savings account?

A. $50-$100

B. $150-$200

C. $200-$250

D. Whatever we have left from paying bills.

8. What is the dollar amount set for birthday and holiday gifts?

A. $50.

B. $300.

C. Under $1,000.00.

D. No limit.

9. We will tithe at our local church?

A. Yes

B. No.

C. Only based on the lower spouse's income.

D. Don't know.

10. Where will we keep our emergency fund?

A. At the house in a safe.

B. Joint savings account.

C. We don't need one.

D. I don't know.

After answering each question you and your spouse should have a clearer understanding of each other's financial view. Don't get discouraged if your answers do not match. It shows you have work to do.

Whether you are single or married a budget is still necessary. One of the questions asked was, who would do the household budget? If you decided that you are then I encourage you to sit your spouse down. Even if she or he doesn't like numbers and finds it difficult, show them in case of an emergency. This will also serve as a great tool when a two income household drops down to one income.

Although we never want to think about it but what if a spouse dies or divorce happens. One spouse is left clueless about any financial records. I do not want this to happen to you. There should be a step by step procedure in place showing how the budget is kept. All listings of account numbers or passwords should be accessible and be stored in a safe place.

Next put a plan in place if one spouse loses their job when the household requires two incomes to cover all household expenses. Would you downsize to a smaller home or even sell the current one you live in? Would one spouse require getting a second job until the other regains employment? This is why saving and getting out debt is vital.

You never know what the future holds if you are not taking control of your money now.

Often times I hear, "What if my spouse doesn't stick to the budget set in place?" Well, a budget is only good as the goal. Communication about the common goal is ongoing. What I like to tell people is to make a vision board and have it visible.

Write the vision, make it plain. (Habakkuk 2:2).

What is a vision board? A vision board is a collage of images, pictures, and affirmations of your dreams and goals. It is the forerunner that will keep your motivation going to achieve your goals. If you have a vision to purchase that dream home, with cash of course, then cut a beautiful home out and post it to your vision board. This will keep you focused.

Don't forget to have fun during your financial freedom movement. There's a list of things you can do for free and stay in your budget such as: picnics, late night walks, bike riding, dancing in the back yard, and movie night.

Once the honeymoon is over be sure to update the following. Circle the ones with no as the answer and work on them.

- Purchase life insurance.
- Update your beneficiary on your life insurance policy.
- Have you updated your existing 401K with your new spouse as the beneficiary?
- Are there living wills in place?
- Discuss filing jointly or marriage filing separately on your taxes.
- Is there a retirement plan in place?

As you plan for your future together enjoy every moment knowing you are taking steps to have complete control over your money.

Authors Words

I pray this book will help you identify and provide solutions to your personal financial needs. I would like to think the activities were helpful based on the purpose of this book and it also established behavior change and renewed your mind. We are recession proof. We can live in the land of overflow with financial freedom. We can have our heart's desire. We have the power to take control of our money one step at a time. I have enough faith that we all can create the life we want on our own terms. All we have to do is believe it, see it, and receive it.

God has given us all everything necessary for life (2 Peter 1:3) NIV. We must unlearn that we will always be broke or we work to pay bills. This involves renewing your mind about your relationship with money. So begin to read your daily affirmation that you established in the beginning of the book. Remember "***It's Your Move Make it Count***".

Contacting the Author

You can contact the author by the following:

Website: www.hayesfinancialcoaching.com

Email: delshawnhayes@yahoo.com

Twitter: @Hayesdel

Instagram: msdrhayes

Acknowledgements

To my best friend Anjoli who has played a major part in helping me to complete this project. May God return your faithfulness as a friend; who has challenged me, inspired me, and encouraged me.

To my wonderful siblings, family, church, and friends who are always cheering me on and always are allowing me to be me.

To Meichelle who inspired me to turn my knowledge and experiences into a book. Yes, I will see you at the top.

To my Editor Cynthia L. Hatcher who was excited about my idea and with joy took on this project to make my dream come into reality.

If I left anyone out please charge it to my mind not my heart.

I love each of you on purpose!

Made in the USA
Monee, IL
04 November 2026

67379779R00049